Your UCAS Application 2014-2015

A Step-by-Step Guide

188521   378-42   COURSES
          ETT.

Contents

Introduction

Completing a UCAS application form is often the first encounter with accurate form filling in you will experience. Much of the form is completed using common sense, but it is easy to trip into pitfalls when you are anxious that your application must be perfect. In this short booklet, I shall guide you every step of the way to completing your application accurately and advise on the Personal Statement.

Of course, you will have experienced tutors to guide you, but you can help yourself to an excellent application in many ways, thus making yours, and your UCAS coordinator's, task straightforward.

You can begin your application as soon as UCAS Apply for your application year becomes live, usually in June, and the more you get done before applications can be submitted in September, the easier it will be to make the final submission.

Things you can do in preparation

Well before September you should be:

- Looking at and familiarizing yourself with the UCAS Website.

- Reading university prospectuses, university websites and books about Higher Education.

- Using the books in your school/college library that detail higher education courses, to help you to choose the best and most suitable course and university for you.

- Finding out when university Open Days are and attending them (with your school's permission if it's in term-time).

- Reading around the subject you wish to study.

- Making notes of the books, newspapers, magazines you have read about your subject choice.

- Looking out for taster courses and lectures and attending some of them.

- Watching plays, films and television programmes – which may be relevant to your course.

- Looking out for relevant essay competitions to enter, and entering them.

An absolute must for all applicants is to acquaint yourself with the UCAS website: http://www.ucas.com

Deadlines

There are three application deadlines for courses through UCAS - 15 October, 15 January and 24 March - it is important to check the deadline for your chosen course(s). If you are applying from the UK, you should submit your application by the relevant deadline below.

15 October 18.00 UK time - deadline for the receipt at UCAS of applications for all medicine, dentistry, veterinary medicine and veterinary science courses (course codes A100, A101, A102, A103, A104, A105, A106, A300, A200, A201, A202, A203, A204, A205, A206, A400, D100, D101 and D102), and for all courses at the universities of Oxford and Cambridge.

15 January 18.00 UK time- application deadline for the receipt at UCAS of applications for all courses except those listed above with a 15 October deadline, and art and design courses with a 24 March deadline.

24 March 18.00 UK time – application deadline for some art and design courses.

6 May – you must reply to any offers by this date (excepting Extra) or they will be assumed declined

2 July – last day to apply through Extra

It is advised that you apply as early as possible. Universities and colleges do not guarantee to consider applications they receive after 15 January, and some popular courses may not have vacancies after that date.

If you are **not** applying to the University of Oxford or the University of Cambridge, you may want to submit your application after the 15 October as the universities you have applied to will know that you are not an Oxbridge candidate.

If you are applying through a sixth-form college, school or centre, you will be given a **buzzword** which you need to enter when registering as it links your application to the establishment, thus enabling your referee to write and add a reference to support your application.

Remember that once you have completed your part of the application, your school/college needs to write and add your reference, which may take a while, so make sure you have 'done your bit' in plenty of time - at least fourteen days before you want to submit your application.

DO NOT MISS YOUR DEADLINE

Getting Started

To get started, just do an internet search for UCAS or go to: http://www.ucas.com.

Once on the UCAS website, choose **Apply** and this will take you to the application page. Under **UCAS Undergraduate** choose *Apply* and this will take you to the page with the icon for applying for your course.

Lots more helpful information can be found on these early pages, take the time to study them.

UCAS Apply is available 24 hours a day and wherever you have online access, you can use the site and work on your application.

You first need to **Register**, using your buzzword, and then you can create your own password. Your school or college may have given you a temporary one which you can change should you wish to.

Always make sure, when completing a 'name' field that you use the name that is on your examination entries and GCSE/AS certificates.

KEEP YOUR USER NAME AND PASSWORD SAFE – and try not to forget them. If you do forget your password, your UCAS co-ordinator should be able to help you to re-set it.

You are now ready to begin.

Page 1 of your application asks for personal details, which are easy and straightforward and many answers have a drop-down menu to select from. However, mistakes are often made.

Title: - be sensible, Mr/Miss/Ms but don't try to be clever and put Dr – this is a legal document and must be filled in accurately.

Gender: - Male or Female

Your first/given name(s): - must be the one(s) on your birth certificate, if you are called Thomas, don't put *Tommy – you can do that later under 'preferred first name'.

Surname/family name: again, this must be the one on your birth certificate or other legal document – your present **legal** surname.

Preferred first name: This is where you can put your preferred name (*Tommy)

Previous surname at 16th birthday: – no need to complete this unless you have changed your name by deed poll, adoption or marriage, etc.

Postal address: this is your current address - don't forget to use capital letters for road names, place names, etc.

Is this your permanent home in the UK?: Yes or No answer.

Home address: no need to complete this if it is the same as your postal address and you have put 'Yes' when asked: **Is this your permanent home in the UK**

Telephone numbers: always worth checking that you have entered them correctly and don't leave them blank.

Email address: Make sure this is a sensible one – you are out to impress the admissions tutors, so don't give a rude or silly address. UCAS will use this to send any messages to you regarding your application, e.g. to say they have received it. If you have a silly email address, set up a sensible one to use for your application.

Date of Birth: ensure what you have put agrees with your birth certificate.

Country of Birth, Date of first entry to UK, Nationality, Dual nationality, Area of permanent residence and Residential Category: these are all straightforward and apart from specifics (e.g. date of first entry to the UK) have drop-down menus.

For example:

Nationality: if you have a UK passport then you select UK National from the drop-down menu.

Reference Numbers

Depending on your school/college, you may not need to fill in any of these, and indeed, may not have these reference numbers. This is where you need to speak with your Tutor/UCAS co-ordinator if in doubt.

Student Support

Fee Code: the majority of applicants will have a Fee Code of 02 – this is where you will be applying for a student loan. Fee Code 01 is for overseas applicants and will incur higher fees. DO NOT put 99 'don't know'.

You also need to add your **Student support arrangements** – this is the authority that will be administering your student finance (loan). There will be a drop down menu to choose from and some areas have a city council as well as a county council – make sure you choose the correct one. If you are unsure, think of who empties your wheelie bin and that will be the correct one. For example, if you live in Leicester, it will be Leicester (City), if you live in Loughborough, then it's Leicestershire. **Please DO NOT leave this blank.**

Don't be worried about having a student loan – it is the best loan you will ever be offered and you will not need to make any re-payments until your salary, after you have graduated, reaches the designated threshold, and even then, it is deducted from your wages in very small amounts (unless you secure highly paid employment, in which case, you will be able to afford larger re-payments). You can find out more from the Student Loans Company website: http://www.slc.co.uk

Don't think of it as a debt, think of it as an investment.

Mailings from UCAS

Here you can choose if, what and how you would like to receive information.

Nominated access: few applicants complete this; it is only for if you would like someone else to speak on your behalf. If you do, you need to add their name and relationship.

Criminal Convictions: you must complete this – and be careful not to put 'Yes' if the answer is 'No'. If it is 'Yes', however, you must be honest.

Disability/Special needs: You must complete this section, even if you do not have a disability, and if this is the case, then choose 'none' from the drop-down menu. If you do have a disability, e.g. dyslexia, you need to give details of any special needs you may have. This will help the university to look after you.

Additional Information

This section is exactly that and, in most cases, much of it is left blank. The questions are straightforward. This information is not used for selection purposes and only used for producing statistical information. It isn't compulsory and you don't have to fill it in.

You can select 'I prefer not to say' as an answer, if you wish to, for any of these questions.

As regards 'educational background' - this refers to your parent or guardian.

Summer Schools and other courses can be included and if you are going to refer to them in your Personal Statement then enter them here too.

Choices

Over the summer, and possibly even long before then, you will have been researching courses you would like to apply for. You can choose up to five courses and the universities/colleges won't see where else you are applying until after you reply to any offers you may get. If you only apply for one course, the fee is halved.

If you are applying for medicine, dentistry, veterinary medicine or veterinary science, you may only have four choices; your fifth might be something like biological sciences, which is good back-up, as these courses are notoriously difficult on which to secure a place.

You may only apply to one course at either the University of Oxford or the University of Cambridge – but check the University websites for more information. When entering your chosen courses, you will need to know the university reference number (e.g. University of Southampton is S27), the name of the course and its code (e.g. English and Music (QW33) and the correct start date. You will be asked 'Live at home?' – ensure you enter 'yes' or 'no' correctly because if you say 'yes' by mistake and you need accommodation, there may not be any available later on. You will also need to say if it is a deferred entry, which will correlate with the start date. You can enter them in any order, as they will be sorted alphabetically anyway.

If you intend to take a gap year, make sure you put 'yes' for deferred entry and don't forget to mention it in your Personal Statement.

Previous UCAS number if known – self-explanatory.

Education

Enter your present school/college, your starting date and the date you will officially leave (NOT *Present*) – it is usually the last day of the summer term.

If you have changed schools and took your GCSE subjects at a different one, then you need to enter the previous school too with accurate starting and leaving dates.

Don't guess at any dates – find out the proper ones.

List your A2 subjects as 'pending' and enter the date of the A-level results day, usually mid-August. If you put June, then there will be no results for UCAS to collect, **it must be the results date**.

Your GCE Advanced subsidiary results may be pending, if you haven't taken them, and again the date will need to be the same as the A2 results day. If you have AS grades, they must be declared.

Enter ALL your GCSE results, even if they are, in your opinion, not very good. The fact is, that is the result and it has to be declared.

Enter any IGCSE results you may have and any music qualifications and Duke of Edinburgh Awards.

For other qualifications you need to click on *other qualification type not in this list'* for example, GNVQ, BTec, etc.

The more you can include, the better it is for you. Don't be shy.

Your Tutor or UCAS co-ordinator may wish to see your certificates – they will have to tick a box to confirm that they have checked the results you have entered and that they are correct.

In this section you may have to include additional entrance tests such as LNat for Law and BMat or Ukcat for Medicine.

Employment

If you have had any type of paid employment – Saturday job, holiday work, etc. add it in – this shows you to be reliable and responsible, and it is important if the employment is relevant to your chosen course. For voluntary work or work experience, include in your Personal Statement.

THE PERSONAL STATEMENT

This is your showcase opportunity to tell your chosen universities why you want to study there, the reasons for choosing the course and what a great student you would be!

You have 4,000 characters in which to do this – please don't try and write more, as anything above will not show up on the application.

Don't type straight on to the application, use a word document so that you can edit and spell-check before pasting in the final version.

You must use your personal statement to make the best impression you can on Admissions Tutors.

It should be exactly what the title indicates: - PERSONAL

To make the statement outstanding you will need to:

Show genuine enthusiasm for the course(s) you have chosen.

Show what motivates you to your choice of study.

Show academic enthusiasm.

(Hopefully, you will have already demonstrated this to your school/college and the enthusiasm for your chosen course should also be evident in their reference.)

Show more than the absolutely academic. Universities want to know about you and what kind of person you are – give the Admissions Tutors insights into your personality by telling them of your interests, achievements and any relevant work experience.

Show them that you are an accomplished individual: you need to give as complete a picture of yourself as possible. You may be called for interview and the statement will play an important part in the university's decision. It will certainly play a part in the selection of questions you may be asked.

If/when you are called for interview, make sure you ask for a copy of your application, including the school reference, to read beforehand and to take with you – **be prepared**.

When thinking about your chosen course(s), consider what it is that inspires you about it? Ask yourself the following:

- Why do you enjoy the subject you have chosen to study, or if it's a new subject for you, why do you believe you will benefit from it, and how?

- Which aspects of it are you most keen on?

- What theories would you enjoy putting into practice? Be specific.

- What is it that specifically interests you about the subject that you would like to explore in greater depth?

- What skills can you bring to the course?

- How did work experience help, if you have done any?

You might decide that you do not need to address all of these questions in the final version of your statement – but these are the kind of questions that you must ask yourself in the initial draft; write the answers down for when you shape your final presentation.

Some Helpful suggestions:

Devote 60-65% of your statement to exploring, explaining and extolling the course you intend to follow, without sucking up too much.

You must make your application stand out - it needs to be fresh, original and different from the crowd. Begin with the influence of your present studies, but look beyond them to include wider reading and research. When you are in your final year as an undergraduate, you will look back on your A levels in a similar way you now think of your GCSEs. Your outlook should not be limited by your present course of study.

Don't simply say: '*I have read Paul Fussell's book on The First World War.*' It would be better to instead write something like: "I particularly enjoyed Chapter V of Paul Fussell's book, *The Great War and Modern Memory,* entitled *Oh What a Literary War in* which he 'examines the collision between events and the language available to describe them.' It is an inspired way of writing about the War and the literature it brought forth. I do feel that although some aspects of the book are dated, it is essential reading for anyone wishing to understand British World War 1 fiction and poetry."

Don't open your statement with a quote – if you are going to use quotes, make sure they are relevant to your course and not just to prove a point.

By doing this, you display skills which make you attractive to your proposed Faculty, those of evaluation, analysis and argument. You present yourself as an independent learner.

In the final 30% of your statement, you can talk about your other interests and extra-curricular activities. Always remember that universities can be highly sensitive political bodies. Don't over-do the leadership roles and keep the tone good-humoured and sensible. You may be Captain of the football team, a marathon runner, an amateur dramatist or an NCO in a cadet force, but the university is selecting you as a student. Will you get your essays in on time if every afternoon is spent on the sports field or at theatre rehearsals?

Never be afraid of re-writing a phrase, sentence or paragraph over and over again. The statement must have your identity: don't be afraid to change things as your confidence in writing the statement grows.

Always remember: what you write as an initial draft is not set in stone. The only point of no-return is after the 'send' button has been pressed and your application has gone to UCAS.

Extra

Extra opens on 25 February until 2 July and if it applies to you, it will show up when you log in to track your application.

If you haven't been made an offer for any of your five chosen courses, or if you have declined them, then you may be able to use *Extra* to add another choice.

If you didn't use all five choices then you can add more in *Track,* providing you have not accepted or declined your offer, it's before 30 June and as long as you originally only applied for one course. You can pay the extra £11 in Track and add more.

Where can it all go wrong?

Providing you have checked that you have completed the first part of the application correctly, it will all be down to the Personal Statement. This is frequently the weakest, and often badly executed, section of a UCAS application.

What are the signs of a bad personal statement?

Considering how important the statement is, the most irritating and annoying weakness is outright carelessness.

Sloppy presentation and content.
Remember, you are writing a serious and professional 'job' application.
Weak applicants misjudge the tone of their statement – you should stay focused and don't state the obvious; it wastes your allotted characters.

Lack of structure.
Your statement must be well thought-out, logical and as comprehensive as possible. Too many weak applicants don't seem to know what to write or show no evidence of ordered planning.

Too short.
Make the most of the space available: 4,000 characters (including spaces) or 47 lines of text (including blank lines). Being too brief might make you sound uninteresting. Keep referring to your initial outpouring and pull in the most interesting parts. But don't waffle on just to fill space.

Poor spelling and grammar.
Checking spelling and grammar is essential. Ask other people to go over it with a fine-tooth comb. Admissions Tutors will assume it to be your highest standard of work.

Dullness.
Your statement must show the Admissions Tutors that you are an interesting individual and how enthusiastic you are about your chosen course. Don't start by saying "from a young age I have always enjoyed ….." or "President Kennedy said…" Think of something more original – you need an exceptional 'hook line' which doesn't begin with 'I'.

Underselling.
Admissions Tutors like to see somebody who has a fully-developed personality in all aspects. Your interests and achievements outside the academic are also important, especially if they show reliability, commitment, and recognised achievements, such as Music grades and Duke of Edinburgh Awards.

Truth and Lies.

If you are asked to go to one of your chosen universities for interview, they will want to talk about your Personal Statement. Please don't fabricate any claims of achievement or declare an interest in something just because you think that is what they want to hear. You must be absolutely certain that your declarations are genuine.

Generalisation.

Present your statement with depth. For example, don't say simply that you are interested in Music, state what kind of music you favour and why you like it as opposed to a different kind.

Plagiarism.

Never, ever be tempted to copy someone else's statement, even if it's a long time ago since they applied. Never cut-and-paste from the Internet; apart from the dubious morality of such practice, using someone else's words isn't effective and will make your statement sound shallow or false. You need to stamp **your** identity on **your** statement. Plagiarism software can be used to identify copied or stolen wording and your school or college will be informed if it is detected.

Nearly all of these pitfalls can be avoided.

Write yourself some rules – here are a few to get you started:

Rule 1:   Start early

Rule 2:   Stay focused

Rule 3:   Check your spelling and grammar

Rule 4:   Be specific

When you are completely satisfied that your application is complete, you must tick all the boxes for "Pay and Send". Once you have done this, the application is in the hands of your Tutor/UCAS co-ordinator and you cannot make any further changes. However, you can ask for it to be unlocked and returned to you should you need to.

Check with your school/college about payment. Some schools pay for your application and you then reimburse them, some prefer you to pay online – **you do need to check**. To apply for multiple courses (up to five) the cost is £23 and £12 if you are only applying for one course. Applications sent after 30 June are £23.

You will receive an email from UCAS when they receive your application with a passcode for using *Track*.

Personal details

Personal

Title	Mr
Gender	Male
First/given name(s)	Andy – wrong! Andrew – as on your birth certificate
Surname/family name	Capp
Preferred first name	Andy – correct
Previous surname at 16th birthday	Capp – wrong! No need to complete unless there has been a legal change
Postal address	1 High Street, Smalltown, Anyshire, SM1 3GG
Is your permanent home in the UK?	Yes
Home address	No need to complete this unless it is different from your Postal Address
Home telephone number	
Mobile number	07779 6005$$ (you need to put one contact number at least)
Email address	Andy.Capp@Gmail.com - must be sensible
Date of birth	5 August 1957 this must be the same as your birth certificate
Country of birth	England
Date of first entry to UK	Leave blank unless you are an overseas student
Nationality	British (check passport if unsure)
Dual nationality	Only complete this if you do have dual nationality (i.e. a passport for another country as well)
Area of permanent residence	Anyshire
Residential category	UK Citizen or EU National check if unsure

Reference numbers You will probably leave these blank – check with your school or college.

Unique Learner Number (ULN)	
Independent Safeguarding Authority (ISA) Number	
Test of English as a Foreign Language (TOEFL) Number	
International English Language Testing System (IELTS) TRF Number	

Student support

Fee code	01 Private finance- **Wrong**! (Unless you are non-UK resident) use **02** otherwise you will be paying the higher rate fees DO NOT put 99-don't know!
Student support arrangements	Anyshire – make sure this is correct (wheelie-bin!)

Mailings from UCAS

Do you want to receive information by text message?	No
Do you want to receive information by email?	No
Do you not want to receive information by post?	Yes These answers mean you won't receive anything from UCAS at all

Nominated access Don't complete this unless you want someone else to speak on your behalf

Full name of nominee	Florrie (Flo) Capp remove
Relationship to you	Friend and life partner remove

Criminal convictions

Criminal convictions	No take care here! And be honest.

Disability/special needs

Category	You have a mental health condition, such as depression, schizophrenia or anxiety disorder
Please give details of any special needs	Check UCAS website for guidelines

Additional information

This section is not used for selection purposes

Ethnic origin

National identity

Dual national identity

Activities in preparation for higher education: 1

Sponsor

Start date

Duration (days)

School year

Location

Activities in preparation for higher education: 2

Sponsor

Start date

Duration (days)

School year

Location

Have you been in care?	No
Duration in care	
Parental education	
Occupational background	Rent Collector
I would like correspondence from Welsh universities, colleges and UCAS to be in Welsh	No

Choices

Brunel University (B84)

English and Music (QW33)

Campus: Main Site (-)	Live at home while studying?: Yes
	Make sure you only put yes if you are definitely going to live at home – **NO** if you will need accommodation
Start date: September 2015	Deferred entry?: Yes - Wrong
	Point of entry: Usually left blank

Brunel University (B84)

Journalism (P500)

Campus: Main Site (-)

Start date: September 2016

Live at home while studying?: No

Deferred entry?: Yes - correct

Point of entry:

University of Cambridge (C05)

Anglo-Saxon, Norse, and Celtic (QQ59)

Campus: Christ's (A)

Start date: October 2015

Live at home while studying?: No

Deferred entry?: No

Point of entry:

Oxford University (O33)

Sanskrit (3 years) (Q450) You can't apply to Oxford if you are applying to Cambridge

Campus: Balliol (O)

Start date: October 2016

Live at home while studying?: No

Deferred entry?: Yes

Point of entry:

University of Southampton

English and Music (QW33)

Campus: Main Site (-)

Start date: September 2015

Live at home while studying?: No

Deferred entry?: No

Point of entry:

Previous UCAS application number (if known)

Education

Please state the highest level of qualification you expect to have before you start your course

Below honours degree level qualifications unless you are applying to do a post-graduate course

Daily Mirror Academy (6$$22, 02/2009 - 06/2015, FT) WRONG! Leaving date should be the last day of the summer term

GCE Advanced Level

Business Studies	08/2015 AQA
English Literature	08/2015 AQA
Music	08/2015 OCR

Don't forget to include General Studies if you will be taking the exam.

GCE Advanced Subsidiary (first award 2001)

History	08/2015 OCR

GCSE

Biology	D 08/2013 AQA
English Language	E 08/2013 AQA
English Literature	B 08/2013 AQA
French	C 08/2013 OCR
History Syllabus B	C 08/2013 OCR
Music	C 08/2013 OCR
Spanish	B 08/2013 WJEC

Employment

Barman – Jack's place
Say what your responsibilities were

Personal statement

This is your showcase to impress – 4,000 characters to make an impact

Date(s) unavailable

You cannot complete this, but if you are going to be unavailable at any time, please tell your UCAS co-ordinator so that they can enter the dates.

PAY AND SEND

Don't forget to complete this section otherwise your reference can't be added.

The rest of the application will be completed by your Tutor/UCAS co-ordinator, including your reference and predicted grades.

Don't forget, you can check everything on the UCAS website: http://www.ucas.com

What are you waiting for?

You can use the following pages to jot down your ideas for completing a perfect UCAS application.

Notes on Reading:

General Notes:

Personal Statement

Notes for the opening paragraph and first 60/65% of the statement

Notes for the final 30/35%

4,000 characters (including spaces) or 47 lines of text (including blank lines)

Applying to
U.K.
Universities
Through
UCAS

By Karen Ette, M.A.

Karen Ette has worked in educational administration for over twenty years and has helped hundreds, (thousands even) of pupils to correctly complete their UCAS applications. This booklet shares the experience gathered during those years.